CHIEF FLYING HAWK'S TALES

The True Story of Custer's Last Fight

As told by Chief Flying Hawk

to

M. I. McCreight (Tchanta Tanka)

ALLIANCE PRESS

PUBLISHERS   NEW YORK

PRINTED IN THE UNITED STATES OF AMERICA

<u>Printing Statement:</u>

Due to the very old age and scarcity of this book,
many of the pages may be hard to read due to the
blurring of the original text, possible missing pages,
missing text and other issues beyond our control.

Because this is such an important and rare work, we
believe it is best to reproduce this book regardless of
its original condition.

Thank you for your understanding.

Chief Flying Hawk at 62.

FOREWORD

As Troop Commander, Headquarters Troop, 7th Cavalry, U. S. Army, stationed at Fort Bliss, Texas, I am interested in the completion of history outlining the misfortunes this Regiment encountered while under the command of General Custer at the battle of Little Big Horn. I have read the manuscript of the old Indian Chief telling his experiences, in company with his cousin, Crazy Horse, in that historic affair. It is something new, and I think it is important because it helps clear up the fog of mystery, which for sixty years, has clouded the happenings and sustained the controversy regarding that unfortunate military disaster.

It is well known that Crazy Horse had a leading part in the fight; he led the Sioux in nearly every contest with U. S. Troops during the strenuous days following the Bozeman Trail troubles, and he was never conquered; his fame increases with the passing of time; for him the only monument erected by the Government, was placed recently, to mark the spot where he met a sad and untimely death, at Fort Robinson. Cousin and constant chum of the war chief, the author of this account of the fight gives us a story that merits the serious consideration of every fair-minded reader.

Personal acquaintance with the author of the book; his early day experiences on the frontier; his intimate acquaintance and long intercourse with Indians, justifies me in believing that a grateful public will read Flying Hawk's Tales with more than ordinary delight and satisfaction.

JOHN P. SCOTT,
Captain, 7th Cavalry.

Fort Bliss, Texas, April, 1936.

CONTENTS

ILLUSTRATIONS

RED CLOUD

Taken about 1905 by Felix, son of the Chief Flying Hawk, showing Pipe and Pouch sent to the author. Rare picture of the famous old chief taken shortly before his death.

CHIEF FLYING HAWK'S TALES

IN the spectacular street parades of the Great Wild West Shows of old days Buffalo Bill mounted a beautiful white horse to lead the procession. Alongside of him, mounted on his pinto pony, rode Flying Hawk in full regal style, carrying his feathered guidon erect and fluttering in the breeze, while his eagle-quill bonnet not only made a fitting crown but dangled below the stirrups of his saddle. Scalp locks decorated his buckskin war-shirt, and beaded moccasins adorned his feet, for this was the becoming dress for, and carried out the dignity of his high office of Chief on gala day affairs.

After the death of the great Scout the old chief travelled with Colonel Miller's 101 Ranch Shows, and for a time with the Sells-Floto Shows, for it was a relief from the hum-drum life in a two-room log cabin in the desolate Bad Lands country.

It was during one of his last trips with the big circus that the writer telegraphed to the manager, while stationed at a city in an adjoining state, asking him to put the old chief on the train which would bring him for a few days' visit at the Wigwam, where for many years he had so much enjoyed similar visits. Shortly a reply came. The message read: "Coming. Flying Hawk." The writer's car was there to meet him. Thunderbull, the interpreter, had come with him, for the Chief was ill and they feared to trust him to travel alone. He was driven to a doctor's office for an examination and the physician ordered him to be taken to the hospital, saying he was threatened with pneumonia and must have

11

careful attention. He had been travelling in New England
and Canada, and the weather had been cold and wet, which,
with the war-dancing, buffalo-chasing and rough-riding, was
telling on the health of the old man, now 76. When in-
formed of the doctor's decision, the chief remonstrated; he
told of Iron Tail, his old friend, who had been placed in a
hospital under exactly similar conditions a dozen years ago,
and was sent home in a casket. No, he said, he would not
go to the hospital, but wished to go to the Wigwam, where
he could be with his friends and those who knew and understood him.

At the Wigwam he was at home; he liked the cooking and
the sunshine and the open fields and woods, good water, a
little sherry wine now and then, and the fresh pure air that
was sifted through a mile of green forests seemingly for his
benefit. The old man declined all the luxury provided for
him in the way of soft mattress, guest-room, bath, rockers
and springs, and asked to have the shaggy buffalo robes and
blankets put at his disposal on the open veranda. There he
made his couch and slept in the starlight, to be wakened by
the songbirds and the rising sun peeping from the mountain-
tops fifteen miles away.

A couple of days of this change to new environment over-
came the threatened breakdown, and the Chief showed signs
of returning health and vigor. He said he would soon be in
the long sleep with Red Cloud and Sitting Bull, and he would
now talk about Crazy Horse, and tell all about the Custer
fight if the white chief would want it for a paper talk; Thunderbull would help him put it in the white man's words, if the
white Chief would write it as he said.

For years the old Chief had been importuned by newspaper reporters and by magazine and feature writers to give

his own account of what actually took place at the Custer fight, for it was known that he was with Crazy Horse through-out the whole affair and knew more than anyone else about it, but he always declined to be interviewed.   Now he was ready to talk, for he had turned over the old ceremonial peace pipe to his friend after fifty years' possession—since Sitting Bull's reign—and he now wished him to have also the history of his life, and the true story of the Custer fight before he went to the last long sleep.

And so, on the broad veranda, where the old man could look out into the mountains where the deer and the bears still lived, and where nearby he could see the railroad and high-way traffic as overhead roared the airplanes between New York and San Francisco, comfortable chairs and tables, with writing materials, were provided to take down the old Chief's statements exactly as he uttered them in the Lakota dialect and sign language, fully translated by Thunderbull, verified by the chief himself and signed with his thumb-print and by him pronounced "Washta."

THE STORY OF CHIEF FLYING HAWK'S LIFE

"I WAS born four miles below where Rapid City now is, in 1852, about full moon in March.

"My father was Black Fox and my mother's name was Iron Cedarwoman.

"My father was a chief. In a fight with the Crows he was shot below the right eye with an arrow; it was so deep that it could not be pulled out, but had to be pushed through to the ear.

"My tribe was the Ogalalla clan. Our family roamed on hunts for game and enemies all about through the country and to Canada. My father died when he was eighty years old. He had two wives and they were sisters. My mother was the youngest and had five children. The other wife had eight children, making thirteen in all. Kicking Bear was my full brother, and Chief Black Fox was my half brother and was named for our father.

"When ten years old I was in my first battle on the Tongue River—Montana now. It was an Overland Train of covered wagons who had soldiers with them. The way it was started, the soldiers fired on the Indians, our tribe, only a few of us. We went to our friends and told them we had been fired on by the soldiers, and they surrounded the train and we had a fight with them. I do not know how many we killed of the soldiers, but they killed four of us.

"After that we had a good many battles, but I did not take

14

IRON TAIL

The celebrated Chief whose head is on the United States nickle, at age of 64.   The
man of whom Buffalo Bill said to the author: "He is the finest man I know, bar none."

any scalps for a good while. I cannot tell how many I killed when a young man.

"When I was twenty years old we went to the Crows and stole a lot of horses. The Crows discovered us and followed us all night. When daylight came we saw them behind us. I was the leader. We turned back to fight the Crows. I killed one and took his scalp and a field glass and a Crow neck-lace from him. We chased the others back a long way and then caught up with our own men again and went on. It was a very cold winter. There were twenty of us and each had four hourses. We got them home all right and it was a good trip that time. We had a scalp dance when we got back.

"We soon moved camp. One night the Piegans came and killed one of our people. We trailed them in the snow all night. At dawn we came up to them. One Piegan stopped. The others went on. We surrounded the one. He was a brave man. I started for him. He raised his gun to shoot when I was twenty feet away. I dropped to the ground and his bullet went over me; then I jumped on him and cut him through below the ribs and scalped him. We tied the scalp to a long pole. The women blacked their faces and we had a big dance over it.

"The next day I started out again with some men and we ran into a Crow camp. We got into that camp by moonlight, but we got caught. They started to fire on us. We all ran into a deep gulch. We got out, but when it was day we saw them coming with a herd of horses, going back to the Crow camp. We got in front of them and hid in a hollow. When I looked out I saw they had Sioux horses which they had stolen from our camp.

"A big Crow was ahead and the others were riding behind.

I took a good aim at the big Crow and shot him in the chest.
The rest of them left the horses and ran away. The big
Crow was still living. I took another shot at him, then I
took his scalp. We took all the horses they had stolen.
There were sixty-nine head that time.

"Some time after we went to hunt buffalo. All the men
went on this hunt. While we were butchering the kill some
Piegans were coming. We went to meet them and had a
fight. Some missed their horses and were running on foot.
I was on a good fast horse. I ran over one and knocked
him down and fell on him and scalped him alive (ugh).
Another one of my people was close by and he shot the one
I scalped. This fight was below where Fort Peck is.

"More Piegans came. More of them than us. We were
attacked by the Piegans. I kneeled down beside a sage
bush. A Piegan shot at me but missed. I shot at him and
hit his horse. It went down. Then I turned back and
ran into a Piegan. Four of them were butchering buffaloes.
I shot at them but missed. The Piegans ran and left their
horses, and I took them all. We killed three of the Piegans.
They shot one of our horses through the head. The fight
was over and the Piegans went to a hill.

"On the way back we ran into a lot of Crows and we had
a fight on horseback. We chased them but no one was killed.
We had a scalp dance on the Piegans.

"The next fight I remember was when seven of us went on
a hunt of the enemy. We met Crows. The Crows killed
one of our men, and we chased them a long way but got none
of them. We got back.

"Twenty-two of us went out to the head of the Yellowstone
on foot on hunt of the enemy. The Crows saw us first. They
came onto us all at once, yelling and shooting as fast as they

could. They killed one Lakota; they had firearms then. Kicking Bear started after them and I went with him. I took good aim and shot one of their horses. The Crows made a charge on us. We took hiding in the rocks. One boy of our band thirteen years old was shot in the elbow, and one was shot in the back and killed. Another one of our band was shot in the breast but got well. They kept crowding us fast but we kept in the rocks. We made a big yell and started for the Crows. They left their blankets, but we failed to get any of the Crows this time. They had horses but we were on foot, but we got all their blankets and sup- plies. The Crows quit and we buried the boy on the hill among the rocks. We took the wounded man along.

"Next morning we went into a hill to see if any of the enemy was around. We had field glasses then. We saw a band of the Crows killing buffaloes. All had packed up but one. The one not ready yet I took a shot at but missed him. He ran to his horse and jumped on him. The horse was tied to a stake and when he tried to run away the horse fell back from the tied rope and he fell off. We followed him on foot. He was crying. I shot him and he fell. We ran to him. He had a gun ready and before we could scalp him he shot at one of our men and hit him above the knee. I wounded him but he got up and ran. My brother Kicking Bear shot at him and he fell in a hole. He kept shooting at us. Just then a band of Piegans came after us while we were shooting and we had a battle there. Then a big storm came. It got dark and we got away. We got home all right.

"Soon after that I took a band of seven on foot and we went to look for a fight with the Crows. We ran into a big bunch of Crows just below where we fought Custer.

We lay until dark. Then we got into the Big Horn among the timber. We marched single file and stopped along among the trees. I was ahead. I whistled like a whippoorwill. This way we got into the camp of the Crows without raising them. They always kept their horses close to the lodge. We got a bunch of horses and got them away from the camp. I held five of our men to bring the horses. I got a white horse. It had a sheet used for rain. I spread it over myself and the horse. The horse was white too, and so I went back into the Crow camp. I hooted like an owl so the Crows did not know I got back into camp again. I got some more ponies but could get only two of them across the river. I had to swim them over. The other five who had the first lot of horses got them home. We did not see them until we got back and met them at home. That time we got thirty-nine horses.

"On another trip I took twenty-three of my men on foot and went north of Custer field to Bear Buttes—a long way. We camped twenty times. Every morning we went to the highest hill to look out for enemies. On top of a mountain we saw a camp of Piegans. Then we felt something bad would happen. We stuck needles into our arms and cut a slit in them to learn if we would have good luck in a battle. This we did that morning. After that we waited until dark, then we went down to the camp. They were not expecting an enemy and they had their horses all loose. We got among them and whistled like a whippoorwill to keep them quiet. This time we got a lot. There was one Sioux boy that Kicking Bear got a horse for. We travelled all night with the horses. Next morning when it was light we stopped and counted them. We had a hundred and thirty-nine for this trip. We had to travel at night to keep safe.

WILLIAM SPOTTED TAIL

Chief and also President of the Rosebud Indian Association which
sponsored the Sun Dance, 1928. Successor and son of the famous
Chief Spotted Tail.

"In the winter soon after that we started out again. We camped nine times. We travelled early in the morning till late and some days we made thirty miles. Then we got another way and slept without fire. A blizzard came. We could not see and we ran into a camp of Blackfeet Indians. We got three horses, each one, and started right back in the storm. Our tracks were filled with the snow. We got in a creek bed and ran into another camp before we saw them. A woman came out and saw us. She told the camp and they fired on us. The horse I was on was hit. He bucked but I stuck to him and we got home. When we were near home I met my brother Kicking Bear who was going out on the war-path. I turned around and went along again with him and the third one took the horses on home.

"The party of Kicking Bear was thirty-eight, and three turned back. They were going far northwest on the Cannon Ball River. We camped seven times and came to a band of Blackfeet Indians in camp. The Blackfeet are brave and have good nerves. They sneak into Sioux camps and steal our children and take them home and make chiefs of them.

"We waited till it got dark and got close to their camp. One of the Blackfeet coming out alone ran into the Sioux and became scared. He made a fright-noise,—like a wolf scared. We moved back into a hollow place where we could fight. When it was near day we tried to get a bunch of ponies but we could not get away with them. A Blackfoot came out on horse-back onto a hill. We took a shot at him but missed him and hit the horse. I saw the horse fall and ran to him. There was a high bank there and the Blackfoot rolled down it. It was about thirty feet. I stopped at the edge and shot at him but missed him. He shot at me and missed. He got away and I went back into the ravine where the other men were, and the Blackfeet surrounded us. We had a battle there. One of our men got shot in the hip but not killed. We finally ran them off.

"When the great Sioux war came we had lots of battles with the soldiers. We were fighting all the time with Miles and Crook and white soldiers every place we went.

"Some of the Indian agents were honest,—sometimes. Jim McLaughlin's wife was a cousin of my wife. I was not in the fight at Wounded Knee, but was there right after the soldiers shot into our women and children with machine guns and killed so many. The soldiers were wrong. They treated us bad. The army of the white people were afraid of us. They did not like Red Cloud because he talked and told the truth about dishonest agents. They put him in the guardhouse at Fort Robinson and put a stick in his mouth (indicated three inches) and tied his hands so he could not talk when the army officers came to inspect. Sitting Bull was all right but they got afraid of him and killed him. They were afraid of my cousin, Crazy Horse, so they killed him. These were the acts of cowards. It was murder. We were starving. We only wanted food.

"Crazy Horse was my cousin and best friend. A soldier ran a bayonet through his back. He was unarmed, and two other men held him by the arms when the white soldier came behind and put his bayonet through his kidney. I got there a few minutes after he was stabbed. When he was dead his father and brothers took him away and buried him. They never told where he is buried and now we do not know.

"Crazy Horse was never with other Indians unless it was in a fight. He was always the first in a fight, and the soldiers could not beat him in a fight. He won every fight with the whites.

"The young brother of Crazy Horse was on a trip where now is Utah, and there he was killed by some white settlers. They were having some trouble with the Indians there. When Crazy Horse learned that his brother was killed he took his wife with him and went away but told no one where he was going. He was gone for a long time. He went to the place where his brother was killed and camped in the woods where he could see the settlement. He stayed there nine days. Every day he would look around and when he saw some one he would shoot him. He killed enough to satisfy and then he came home. Crazy Horse was married but had no children. He was much alone. He never told stories and never took a scalp from his enemies when he killed them. He was the bravest chief we ever had. He was the leader and the first at the front in the Custer fight. He never talked but always acted first. He was my friend and we went in the Custer fight together.

"I was thirty-two years old when I was made chief. A chief has to do many things before he is chief—so many brave deeds, so many scalps and so many horses.

"Many times I went out to a hill and stayed three days and three nights and did not eat or drink—only just think about the best way to do things for my people.

"When about twenty-six-old I was married. I got two wives. They were sisters. White Day was the name of one, and Goes-Out-Looking was the name of the other one. They belonged to the same tribe but now they are both dead. Only one child. His mother was Goes-Out-Looking and his name Felix. White Day had no child. My years now 76, and soon I will be along with Iron Tail and Red Cloud.

"When my father was dead a long time we went to see how he was on the scaffold where we put him. His bones were all that was left.   The arrow-point was sticking in the back of his skull.   It was rusted.   We took it home with us.

"When my brother, Kicking Bear, died he was put in a grave on a hill.   All his things were put in the grave with him. I will see his son, Kicking Bear, if he will let us dig open the grave and take out the arrow head and send it to this wigwam to put along with my things."

It was late when the old chief completed the telling of the story as above recorded.   He signified a desire for a smoke and the Red Cloud peace-pipe with is long ornamented stem was brought from the cabinet, and some red-willow bark mixed with tobacco for the old-time kinnikinnick, which the chief enjoyed, as between puffs he recalled notable Councils of Treaty with government agents.   He said they always talked with "forked tongues" and did not do as they agreed on in the paper.

After the smoke was over, Thunderbull interpreted his last command.   It was the chief's desire to have a glass of wine and the lights turned out so that he could sleep.   He would tell of the Custer fight tomorrow.

Rain having come on, the robes and blankets were transferred to the sun-porch where he was protected from inclement weather, for, as previously noted, he could not be induced to sleep on a white man mattress and springs.

At sun-up the chief was missing.   Breakfast was delayed. Presently he was seen coming from the forest which nearly surrounds the Wigwam.   In his hand he carried a green switch six feet in length.   From his travelling bag he took a bundle which he carefully unfolded and laid out—a beautiful eagle-feather streamer which he attached to the pole at either end.   After testing it in the breeze, he handed it to his friend with gentle admonishment to keep it in a place where it could always be seen. It was the Chief's "wand," and he said it must always be kept where it could be seen, else the people would not know who was chief. Having disposed of this, to him, important duty, the chief was ready for breakfast.

Rested and refreshed the old sage of the Lakotas was disposed to talk about his people and their unfair treatment through the centuries since Columbus came. It was a fine chance to get the viewpoint of the red man on some episodes in American history that have been told by the white men but about which the Indian has not yet been heard.

Asked about how the red men looked upon the story of John Smith and Pocahontas, the chief proceeded to tell their way of thinking about that romantic tale. He said:

"That Virginia venture was a gold-hunting expedition like when Cortez went to steal from Montezuma the Indian's gold and silver and land. They were a lot of fellows out of a job who wanted to live without work by cheating and robbing the native people who did not have guns.

"Powhatan was kind to them when they came. He gave them food and helped them to make houses to live in. They stayed a long time and did not work and raise food but got it from the Indians. Then when the corn was not plenty for all, Smith told Powhatan that they had been wrecked and soon ships would come from England and take them back home. Ships came and put more English people on the land but did not bring food for them. They were hungry and asked for more corn from the Indians, but there was not enough for all, and so Powhatan told them he had food only for his own people. The white men had guns and swords and told Powhatan he must give them the corn or they would kill his people. Then there was trouble. They took the food from the Indians and the Indians killed some of them and then

they became enemies. It was when they had stolen a lot of
food from the Indians and were in camp to eat it that Smith
said Pocahontas came to them through the path in the woods
and told them the Indians were coming to kill them, and she
put her arms around Smith's neck and cried. It was a good
white man's story, but Indians do not believe it as it is not
their way of killing white men. Smith did not tell this story
until long after he went back to England to put it in his book.
He told a different story before he wrote his book. Pocahontas was a girl only twelve or thirteen years old and Smith was
a hard man more than forty or fifty winters. Rolf took her to
England but she did not live very long there so far away
from her people.

"It was the same with John Smith as it was when Columbus got among the Indians. They liked them and were
friendly as long as the natives gave them food, and then they
tried to take everything they had from them and make slaves
of them to do their work. The Indians did not have the same
kind of God and so they did not treat them like men but
like animals. Columbus made the Indians dig in the mines
for gold, and if they did not find it he killed them, until all of
them on the Island were killed or made slaves for his men."

NEW AMSTERDAM

REFERRING to the purchase of Manhattan for a lot of fish-hooks and trinkets valued at $24, the chief's countenance indicated that it was the best kind of argument to prove how the white men cheated the innocent red folks on every occasion. The Indians had befriended the helpless adventurers when they came among them, and for their kindness the settlers attacked them one night and killed more than a hundred and twenty men, women and children while they were asleep in their wigwams. This was about the first massacre. But it was a white man massacre of Indians. They ran their bay-onets through the stomachs of little babies and flung them out into the river. They cut off the hands of the men and cut open the women with their swords. They went among them with a torch of fire and burned their homes until no Indians were left; and these all were friendly Indians who sold the white people their island for needles, awls and fish-hooks, and brought the furs to them. (This was in 1642 under Kieft's regime.)

The white man's account of this affair tells us that on February 25th at midnight Kieft sent Sergeant Rodolf with a party of soldiers to Pavonia and another party under Adrien-sen to Corlear's Hook where they rushed in upon the sleeping families and killed them all in the most hideous butchery that can be found in American annals.

An eye witness records it in these words: "I remained at the Director's (Kieft) and took a seat in the Kitchen near the fire. At midnight I heard loud shrieks and went out on the parapet of the fort to look—at the flash of guns. I heard no more of the cries of the Indians; they were butchered in their sleep. Sucklings were torn from their mother's breasts, butchered before their mother's eyes and their mangled limbs thrown quivering into the river or the flames. Babes were hacked to pieces while fastened to little boards; others were thrown alive into the river, and when the parents rushed in to save them the soldiers prevented them from landing." De Vries said of it: "some came running to us from the country, having their hands cut off; some lost both arms and legs; some were supporting their entrails with their hands, and mangled in other horrid ways, too horrible to be conceived."

The white man's own history refers to this massacre in the following language: "This crime has hardly a parallel in the annals of savage atrocities, directed as it was, upon a friendly village of harmless, unsuspecting Indians."

But this was merely the beginning of a series of white-man massacres that continued for nearly three centuries.

SITTING BULL

From rare old plate found in Captain Clark's House, Valentine, Nebraska.

THE CUSTER FIGHT

DINNER over, the old man wished to sit on the open veranda in the clear pure air and see the sunset shadows grow slowly over the hills and valleys all about. Another pipe-smoke to get his mind centered properly on the old times, and after a short time of quiet he began to relate the incidents of the Custer fight:

"The Indians were camped along the west side of the Big Horn in a flat valley. We saw a dust but did not know what caused it. Some Indians said it was the soldiers coming. The chief saw a flag on a pole on the hill.

"The soldiers made a long line and fired into our tepees among our women and children. That was the first we knew of any trouble. The women got their children by the hand and caught up their babies and ran in every direction.

"The Indian men got their horses and guns as quick as they could and went after the soldiers. Kicking Bear and Crazy Horse were in the lead. There was thick timber and when they got out of the timber there was where the first of the fight was.

"The dust was thick and we could hardly see. We got right among the soldiers and killed a lot with our bows and arrows and tomahawks. Crazy Horse was ahead of all, and he killed a lot of them with his war-club; he pulled them off their horses when they tried to get across the river where the bank was steep. Kicking Bear was right beside him and he killed many too in the water.

"This fight was in the upper part of the valley where most of the Indians were camped. It was some of the Reno soldiers that came after us there. It was in the day just before dinner when the soldiers attacked us. When we went after them they tried to run into the timber and get over the water where they had left their wagons. The bank was about this high (12 ft. indicated) and steep, and they got off their horses and tried to climb out of the water on their hands and knees, but we killed nearly all of them when they were running through the woods and in the water. The ones that got across the river and up the hill dug holes and stayed in them.

"The soldiers that were on the hill with the pack-horses began to fire on us. About this time all the Indians had got their horses and guns and bows and arrows and war-clubs, and they charged the soldiers in the east and north on top of the hill. Custer was farther north than these soldiers were then. He was going to attack the lower end of the village. We drove nearly all that got away from us down the hill along the ridge where another lot of soldiers were trying to make a stand.

"Crazy Horse and I left the crowd and rode down along the river. We came to a ravine; then we followed up the gulch to a place in the rear of the soldiers that were making the stand on the hill. Crazy Horse gave his horse to me to hold along with my horse. He crawled up the ravine to where he could see the soldiers. He shot them as fast as he could load his gun. They fell off their horses as fast as he could shoot. (Here the chief swayed rapidly back and forth to show how fast they fell). When they found they were being killed so fast, the ones that were left broke and ran as fast as their horses could go to some other soldiers that were further along the ridge toward Custer. Here they tried to make another stand and fired some shots, but we rushed them on along the ridge to where Custer was. Then they made another stand (the third) and rallied a few minutes. Then they went on along the ridge and got with Custer's men.

"Other Indians came to us after we got most of the men at the ravine. We all kept after them until they got to where Custer was. There was only a few of them left then.

"By that time all the Indians in the village had got their horses and guns and watched Custer. When Custer got nearly to the lower end of the camp, he started to go down a gulch, but the Indians were surrounding him, and he tried to fight. They got off their horses and made a stand but it was no use. Their horses ran down the ravine right into the village. The squaws caught them as fast as they came. One of them was a sorrel with white stocking. Long time after some of our relatives told us they had seen Custer on that kind of a horse when he was on the way to the Big Horn.

"When we got them surrounded the fight was over in one hour. There was so much dust we could not see much, but the Indians rode around and yelled the war-whoop and shot into the soldiers as fast as they could until they were all dead. One soldier was running away to the east but Crazy Horse saw him and jumped on his pony and went after him. He got him about half a mile from the place where the others were lying dead. The smoke was lifted so we could see a little. We got off our horses and went and took the rings and money and watches from the soldiers. We took some clothes off too, and all the guns and pistols. We got seven hundred guns and pistols. Then we went back to the women

and children and got them together that were not killed or
hurt.

"It was hard to hear the women singing the death-song for
the men killed and for the wailing because their children were
shot while they played in the camp. It was a big fight; the
soldiers got just what they deserved this time. No good
soldiers would shoot into the Indian's tepee where there were
women and children. These soldiers did, and we fought for
our women and children. White men would do the same if
they were men.

"We did not mutilate the bodies, but just took the valu-
able things we wanted and then left. We got a lot of money,
but it was of no use.

"We got our things packed up and took care of the
wounded the best we could, and left there the next day. We
could have killed all the men that got into the holes on the
hill, but they were glad to let us alone, and so we let them
alone too. Rain-in-the-Face was with me in the fight. There
were twelve hundred of us. Might be no more than one
thousand was in the fight. Many of our Indians were out on
a hunt.

"There was more than one chief in the fight, but Crazy
Horse was leader and did most to win the fight along with
Kicking Bear. Sitting Bull was right with us. His part in
the fight was all good. My mother and Sitting Bull's wife
were sisters; she is still living.

"The names of the chiefs in the fight were: Crazy Horse,
Sitting Bull, Lame Deer, Spotted Eagle and Two Moon. Two
Moon led the Cheyennes. Gall and some other chiefs were
there but the ones I told you were the leaders. The story
that white men told about Custer's heart being cut out is
not true."

HOLLOW HORN BEAR

With his two wives and children, about 1882.   Rare photo by Captain Clark, Scout
with Crook's Army, 1876.

Indicating that he was through, the manuscript was carefully read over to him very slowly in order that he would not
be confused as to the exact meaning of what it contained.
When finished he gave his emphatic approval by hearty "How
How, Washta," and in his expert use of the sign language
directed a pad be brought so that he could place his thumb-
print to show that it was his own sealed document and final
testimony on a subject about which white men have written
countless and varied accounts, all of them being guess-work
based upon circumstantial evidence, for no white man knows.
There were none left to tell just what did occur and how.
The chief was there and he saw and knows. He was last of
the survivors of that historic episode, and it is fortunate that
coming generations could have a truthful and reliable account from him before he too had passed to the happy Hunt-
ing Ground.

THE CHIEF TELLS OF RED CLOUD

RESTED and refreshed, the old Chief desired to talk about the cause of the Custer troubles; he said that Red Cloud was one of their wisest men and knew what was best for his people; he had been their chief for a long time; he tried to keep peace with the whites but it was no use; they would not stay out of the Indian's country, but came and took their gold and killed off all their game. This started the trouble, and the long bloody war with the soldiers came. After the Custer fight, and when the Indians were starving, Red Cloud made a speech about it, he said, and asked to have it read to him now. His host brought from the library a volume containing the talk to which the Chief referred, and it was carefully translated to him by Thunderbull by way of refreshing his memory. On completing this interpretation of Red Cloud's famous address, the Chief directed that it be included in his story of the Custer fight so that people would know why they killed Custer and his troopers. Also, it would tell why there was ghost dancing, and of the massacre at Wounded Knee.

RED CLOUD'S SPEECH

I WILL tell you the reason for the trouble. When we first made treaties with the Government, our old life and our old customs were about to end; the game on which we lived was disappearing; the whites were closing around us, and nothing remained for us but to adopt their ways,—the Government promised us all the means necessary to make our living out of the land, and to instruct us how to do it, and with abundant food to support us until we could take care of ourselves. We looked forward with hope to the time we could be as independent as the whites, and have a voice in the Government.

"The army officers could have helped better than anyone else but we were not left to them. An Indian Department was made with a large number of agents and other officials drawing large salaries—then came the beginning of trouble; these men took care of themselves but not of us. It was very hard to deal with the government through them—they could make more for themselves by keeping us back than by helping us forward.

"We did not get the means for working our lands; the few things they gave us did little good.

"Our rations began to be reduced; they said we were lazy. That is false. How does any man of sense suppose that so great a number of people could get work at once unless they were at once supplied with the means to work and instructors enough to teach them?

33

"Our ponies were taken away from us under the promise that they would be replaced by oxen and large horses; it was long before we saw any, and then we got very few. We tried with the means we had, but on one pretext or another, we were shifted from one place to another, or were told that such a transfer was coming. Great efforts were made to break up our customs, but nothing was done to introduce us to customs of the whites. Everything was done to break the power of the real chiefs.

"Those old men really wished their people to improve, but little men, so-called chiefs, were made to act as disturbers and agitators. Spotted Tail wanted the ways of the whites, but an assassin was found to remove him. This was charged to the Indians because an Indian did it, but who set on the Indian? I was abused and slandered, to weaken my influence for good. This was done by men paid by the Government to teach us the ways of the whites. I have visited many other tribes and found that the same things were done amongst them; all was done to discourage us and nothing to encourage us. I saw men paid by the government to help us, all very busy making money for themselves, but doing nothing for us.

"Now do you not suppose we saw all this? Of course we did, but what could we do? We were prisoners, not in the hands of the army but in the hands of robbers. Where was the army? Set to watch us but having no voice to set things right. They could not speak for us. Those who held us pretended to be very anxious about our welfare and said our condition was a great mystery. We tried to speak and clear up that mystery but were laughed at as children.

"Other treaties were made but it was all the same. Rations were again reduced and we were starving—sufficient food not given us, and no means to get it from the land. Rations were

Top—From left to right: LONE BEAR, AMERICAN HORSE (BEN), IRON TAIL, IRON CLOUD, WHIRLWIND. All Sioux Chiefs, taken by the author in 1908.

Below—CHIEF BLACK THUNDER.

still further reduced; a family got for two weeks what was not enough for one week. What did we eat when that was gone? The people were desperate from starvation,—they had no hope. They did not think of fighting; what good would it do; they might die like men but what would the women and children do?

"Some say they saw the Son of God. I did not see Him. If he had come He would do great things, as He had done before. We doubted it for we saw neither Him nor His works. Then General Crook came. His words sounded well but how could we know that a new treaty would be kept better than the old one? For that reason we did not care to sign. He promised that his promise would be kept—he at least had never lied to us.

"His words gave the people hope; they signed. They hoped. He died. Their hope died with him. Despair came again. Our rations were again reduced. The white men seized our lands; we sold them through General Crook but our pay was as distant as ever.

"The men who counted (census) told all around that we were feasting and wasting food. Where did he see it? How could we waste what we did not have? We felt we were mocked in our misery; we had no newspaper and no one to speak for us. Our rations were again reduced.

"You who eat three times a day and see your children well and happy around you cannot understand what a starving Indian feels! We were faint with hunger and maddened by despair. We held our dying children and felt their little bodies tremble as their soul went out and left only a dead weight in our hands. They were not very heavy but we were faint and the dead weighed us down. There was no hope on earth. God seemed to have forgotten.

"Some one had been talking of the Son of God and said He had come. The people did not know; they did not care; they snatched at hope; they screamed like crazy people to Him for mercy; they caught at the promise they heard He had made.

"The white men were frightened and called for soldiers. We begged for life and the white men thought we wanted theirs; we heard the soldiers were coming. We did not fear. We hoped we could tell them our suffering and could get help. The white men told us the soldiers meant to kill us; we did not believe it but some were frightened and ran away to the Bad Lands. The soldiers came. They said: 'don't be afraid—we come to make peace, not war.' It was true; they brought us food. But the hunger-crazed who had taken fright at the soldiers' coming and went to the Bad Lands could not be induced to return to the horrors of reservation life. They were called Hostiles and the Government sent the army to force them back to their reservation prison."

WOUNDED KNEE

THE old man being assured that Red Cloud's talk would be incorporated in his story of the Custer fight, then said he wished to tell about the massacre of Indians by the white soldiers at Wounded Knee, where, he indicated as his belief, they carried out this slaughter in retaliation for the Custer affair, and proceeded:

"This was the last big trouble with the Indians and soldiers and was in the winter in 1890. When the Indians would not come in from the Bad Lands, they got a big army together with plenty of clothing and supplies and camp-and-wagon equipment for a big campaign; they had enough soldiers to make a round-up of all the Indians they called hostiles.

"The Government army, after many fights and loss of lives, succeeded in driving these starving Indians, with their families of women and gaunt-faced children, into a trap, where they could be forced to surrender their arms. This was on Wounded Knee creek, northeast of Pine Ridge, and here the Indians were surrounded by the soldiers, who had Hotchkiss machine guns along with them. There were about four thousand Indians in this big camp, and the soldiers had the machine guns pointed at them from all around the village as the soldiers formed a ring about the tepees so that Indians could not escape.

"The Indians were hungry and weak and they suffered

from lack of clothing and furs because the whites had driven away all the game. When the soldiers had them all sur- rounded and they had their tepees set up, the officers sent troopers to each of them to search for guns and take them from the owners. If the Indians in the tepees did not at once hand over a gun, the soldier tore open their parfleech trunks and bundles and bags of robes or clothes,—looking for pistols and knives and ammunition. It was an ugly business, and brutal; they treated the Indians like they would torment a wolf with one foot in a strong trap; they could do this be- cause the Indians were now in the white man's trap,—and they were helpless.

"Then a shot was heard from among the Indian tepees. An Indian was blamed; the excitement began; soldiers ran to their stations; officers gave orders to open fire with the machine guns into the crowds of innocent men, women and children, and in a few minutes more than two hundred and twenty of them lay in the snow dead and dying. A terrible blizzard raged for two days covering the bodies with Nature's great white blanket; some lay in piles of four or five; others in twos or threes or singly, where they fell until the storm subsided. When a trench had been dug of sufficient length and depth to contain the frozen corpses, they were collected and piled, like cord-wood, in one vast icy tomb. While separating several stiffened forms which had fallen in a heap, two of them proved to be women, and hugged closely to their breasts were infant babes still alive after lying in the storm for two days in 20' below zero weather."

"I was there and saw the trouble,—but after the shooting was over; it was all bad."—the old chief said.

The host produced an old photo showing the bodies of the victims as they lay scattered and in bunches over the bleak frozen grounds; the Chief looked at it and immediately recognized the body of Big Foot which lay on top of a pile of the dead, face upward. Another photo showing the trench being filled with the dead also showed a number of army officers standing nearby. The Chief readily recognized Frank Gruard, Buffalo Bill, General Miles and Kicking Bear,—his own brother. He shook his head and said, "Wahnitcha"— bad.

SITTING BULL

AS the famed Sitting Bull was his uncle, the chief wished to talk about him, and told of the suffering that followed the removal of the Minnesota bands to Crow Creek in 1863. There the young man learned of the terrible injustices and frightful sufferings that his people were subjected to at the hands of the national government through its grafting agents and hordes of unconcionable politicians. The outrageous treatment of these innocent and confiding natives, whose rich land along the Mississippi was confiscated by the land-speculators—and then "purchased" by treaty, but never paid for, as usual, and the owners thrust far out into the barren sandhills and allowed to starve and die of helplessness and foul disease—left an indelible hate in the heart of Sitting Bull against the white race.

Sitting Bull was a natural leader, but it was after the ruthless breaking by the whites of the treaty of 1868, that he gained wide prominence; he visited Washington with Red Cloud and Spotted Tail, where they were entertained by President Grant.

At a council on Powder River he made a speech to his associates which indicates the range of his oratory and intellect. He said:

"Behold, my brothers, the Spring has come; the earth has received the embraces of the sun and we shall soon see the results of that love!

"Every seed is awakened; and so has all animal life. It is through this mysterious power that we too have our being, and we therefore yield to our neighbors, even to our animal neighbors, the same right as ourselves, to inhabit this land.

"Yet hear me, people, we have now to deal with another race—small and feeble when our fathers first met them, but now great and overbearing. Strangely enough, they have a mind to till the soil, and the love of possession is a disease with them. These people have made many rules that the rich may break, but the poor may not; they have a religion in which the poor worship, but the rich will not. They take tithes from the poor and weak to support the rich and those who rule. They claim this mother of ours, the earth, for their own and fence their neighbors away; they deface her with their buildings and their refuse. That nation is like a spring freshet that over-runs its banks and destroys all who are in its path.

"We cannot dwell side by side. Only seven years ago we made a treaty by which we were assured that the buffalo country should be left to us forever. Now they threaten to take that from us. My brothers, shall we submit, or shall we say to them: 'First kill me before you take possession of my fatherland.'"

Observing a photograph of Sitting Bull which hung on the wall, the old chief remarked that he was the brains of the fighting forces, but the fighting was led by Crazy Horse, his young war-chief. This was after Red Cloud had agreed to peace and retired from active leadership. He said that Sitting Bull was always a fair fighter and never killed any women or children.

Noticing the old ceremonial peace-pipe in the cabinet, which he had presented to the writer after holding it as head chief for half a century, the chief told how it had been turned over to him by Sitting Bull when he left to lead his so-called hostiles to Canada, after the Custer battle. He said most of the great treaties had been made over its smoke, and that it was more than a hundred years old, and probably much older.

Mention of Sitting Bull's life in Canada brought from the old chief the story of a visit he made to Sitting Bull's camp in Wood Mountain long years after the great chief's death; he said:

"When Sitting Bull left for Canada with the hostiles, seven families, who were not of his band, were missed from the reservation; no one knew where they were and they were given up as killed by the whites."

Then about forty years passed and Flying Hawk heard that a band of Indians were living at Sitting Bull's old camping ground in Canada. He went to visit them. He found that they numbered five hundred, and they lived in tepees just as the Indians lived in the old days, and that they had all descended from the original seven lost families. He said they were fine healthy and happy, and their hair reached below the knee.

While talking about Sitting Bull, the old chief referred to his speech about treaties made with the whites. On examination, the library had a volume containing the speech which was read to the old man by the interpreter. He asked to have it placed with his Custer account so that people would know the truth about the way Indians were abused and cheated. The speech follows:

"What treaty that the white man kept has the red man broken? Not one.

TWO STRIKES

Famous old chief of the hostile Sioux. Rare old plate from Captain Clark's house in Valentine, Nebraska, supposed to have been made about 1885.

"What treaty that the white man ever made with us have they kept? Not one.

"When I was a boy the Sioux owned the land; the sun rose and set on their country; they sent ten thousand horse-men to battle! Where are the warriors today? Who slew them? Where are our lands?—Who owns them?

"What white man can say I ever stole his lands or a penny of his gold? Yet they say I am a thief! What white woman, however lonely, was ever a captive or insulted by me? Not one, yet they say I am a bad Indian. What white man has ever seen me drunk? Who has ever come to me hungry and went unfed? Who has ever seen me beat my wives or abuse my children? What law have I ever broken? Is it wrong for me to love my own? Is it wicked for me because my skin is red—because I am a Sioux—because I was born where my fathers lived—because I would die for my people and my country?"

The old chief had "talked enough" he said, and was now ready to go on the long trip to the Black Hills where he would soon lie down for the long sleep. Just now he was feeling better. The doctor's certificate, and a letter to be handed the manager of the show, with a last good bye, and the motor car sped him on his way west.

Chief Flying Hawk died December 24, 1931, at Pine Ridge, South Dakota.

THE LAST SUN DANCE

To get a close-up of present conditions after a long absence from the Sioux country, an invitation to join in the last Sun Dance which was planned to take place in the fall of 1928, was accepted. There was to be a "fifty-years' " celebration at the old Rosebud Agency where the ceremony of the sun dance, stopped by the Government forty-five years ago, was to be performed. All the old-time Indians were to be there.

It required a long night-drive from the railroad station to reach the old post, and there was no hotel, no lighting system. The accommodations consisted of an abandoned officer's house and a cot set up by an amiable boarding house proprietress by the light of a candle. There was neither water, light nor furniture, but plenty of accumulated dust, and it was cold. But breakfast was promised at the boarding house in the morning. When daylight came it proved to be likewise an abandoned structure that one time was a sort of soldiers' barracks. It was sadly in need of repair, for one had to be cautious in walking over the veranda floors to avoid falling through. An orange, bacon and eggs, cakes and fried potatoes were served by a Cheyenne boy and a Sioux girl in the former sitting room, where the two breakfast tables were spread with their red damask covers and ornamented with the circle castors, pea-green service dishes and blue-bordered plates.

44

The landlady was kind-hearted and a good cook, which made up for the many other failures in a first rate hostelry. Anyway we came to see Indians. Nothing else mattered.

Stepping out on the wabbly porch for a look around the old agency compound, a wrinkled old man in slouch hat and white man's discarded coat stood leaning on a long staff. He had part of a loaf of stale bread enclosed in his left arm, held closely as if it was precious, and from it he tore off chunks with his right hand and stuffed them into his mouth and ravenously gulped them down.

It was pathetic to see. Turning to the landlady for an explanation, she said the man was Chief Black Thunder, and she had given him the bread because she could not bear to see him suffering from hunger and cold; he was eighty-four and nearly blind from trachoma. In the brick building across the parade ground, a short distance from the eating place, stood the agency office, and nearby was the commissary and storehouses of the government, representing the nearly two billions of money and property belonging to the Indians, administered by the more than five thousand agents, employees, superintendents and welfare experts of the Indian Bureau, on salaries high and low, much of which was taken from the Indians' funds.

An Indian farmer with his two daughters drove up in a dilapidated Ford. He had some business with the agent, and while absent on that duty the young ladies were interrogated about the big show where it was located and how to get there. For seventy-five cents they would take us to the grounds three miles away. The bargain was closed; down the steep bank, around the curves and up the cliffs on the opposite side of the "river" the rickety car was sent through deep dust, for a first glimpse of the big camp.

From a promontory was witnessed a scene the like of which was never seen before and in all likelihood will not be seen again. Far to the west, beyond the Bad Lands, were the Black Hills, and to the east the lower hills hid the vast plains that roll away to the Missouri. An equal distance north and south once formed a buffalo range where countless herds fed and furnished food, clothing and shelter for the red race, since the coming of the Spanish with horses, at the south.

In a great saucerlike area between the hills were assembled the largest Indian Congress of modern times. They told us that when all had arrived there would be twenty thousand Indians in camp. A thousand or more tepees and tents were scattered about in villages of dozens, fifties and hundreds, over this undulating, parched and dusty threebyfivemile camping area. All around within the range of vision were the horses and ponies in bands large and small pasturing on the sundried grass; they were herded by the youths mounted in cowboy style on their duns and pintos, who kept them constantly rounded up to prevent their too widely straying. Droves of the ponies were being constantly driven to and from the watering place two miles away, where the little river wound its way among the scrubby plum and cottonwood trees below the posttrader's log store.

Everywhere in the open spaces were Indians, old and young; women with papooses on their backs, and dogs, dogs of all sizes and all breeds and colors—they were a part of every family. It was like a white man's country fair; they were having their annual visit before the ceremonies began; coming, going, singly and in crowds or sitting in circles squat on the ground, chatting in their peculiar dialect and signlanguage, of neighborhood affairs and idle gossip. Women,

Chiefs Flying Hawk and Iron Tail, with the author and son in 1911-12. Flying Hawk at left. This son, age five, was a favorite of Iron Tail who claimed him as his "son" and gave him the name Tchanta-Tanka, same as bestowed on the author when adopted—meaning Great Heart. Ages at this time were about 58 and 60.

girls and children were dressed in gorgeous colors; some in white buckskin robes with fancy beadwork; others in brilliant shade of synthetic silk or sateen, and still others in green or red-striped shawls artfully draped about the shoulders. Mostly they were bespangled with gay and sparkling jewelry and strings of beads about the neck and arms. Old-time warriors, bedecked with eagle feathers, fancy moccasins and war-dance regalia, strode about in all their former glory, while here and there an old chief, in scalp-shirt, with the lordly war-bonnet of black-tipped eagle quills reaching to his heels, could be seen in all his stately bearing. It was a thrilling spectacle and brought back memories of frontier times of half a century ago. Artist could not paint, nor is it possible to write, a true description of it or of the tremendous magnitude and meaning of it all.

The open-air stage with its human and animal players stretched away as far as the eye could see. Here were gathered many tribes and clans, the relic of a great race, once possessors of a vast continent—remnant of a race robbed of its God-given heritage—assembled here for the last time to pay homage to their Great Spirit, a ceremony denied to them for forty-five years by their merciless conquerors. Now, with the omission of the self-inflicted tortures, they were to have the right to pay reverence to their God, the sun—symbol of their Supreme Power, source of light, of heat and of all else that lives and has its being on the earth.

Only the old men and women knew and understood the intricacies of the ritual—the others were the product, or shall we say victims, of the white man's civilization.

As the sun went down in dark clouds fringed with orange and gold, and the twilight cast long shadows from the rugged western hills, the strange scene gradually faded and darkness spread over it all. Flash lights and torches appeared and camp-fires were showing all around, like myriad fire-flies flit-ting about in the gloom. A faint roar like the hum of a distant cataract could be heard, broken by the shouts of the herder-boys as they made their nightly round-up. Here and there could be heard the tom-tom and uncanny war-songs of the weird dances and feasts being held in various sections of the great encampment.

Alone on the hill, in the darkness, came the thought that gradually grew into conviction—here was about to open the curtain on the last act of a great world drama.

This great conclave had gathered here from all the country round; they came from Kansas, Oklahoma, Utah, Colorado, Wyoming, Montana, Idaho, Nebraska and North and South Dakota;—they came in wagons, worn-out Fords, and some by train from distant points. They had their camp equip-ment, food, clothing and regalia, with forage for their horses and ponies, with barrels of water for use in camping on the dry and dusty trip over the arid plains and desert country. It was for them an event of a lifetime, and they came and conducted themselves accordingly.

There were few whites present. It was a hard journey for them with their esthetic tastes and habits. It was Indian country, and the government furnishes accommodation only for its employees.

In the center of the big camp grounds had been erected a sun dance pole about forty feet high, to which, about half way up, was attached a bundle of brush with green leaves on the tips, which formed a sort of rude cross. Surrounding this pole, and a hundred feet distant from it, was a double stockade of tree-trunks set on end and connected at the top with smaller but similar materials, and over all were spread green boughs, making a kind of canopy, in the shade of which the older people and guests could sit to watch the performance carried on within the circle.

From one-thirty to four-thirty, or sundown, each day for four days, the ceremonies were performed. Twelve men and five women took part as principals in the sacred sun dance; they dressed in most grotesque costumes, but remained naked from the crown to the waist-line, which they painted in hideous and fantastic colors.

Music for the dancing was furnished by seven old men aged seventy-eight and over, led by Lonefeather, who carried a "discharge" from government scout-service in the late seventies. To the accompaniment of the weird yelps and chanting of these old men they tapped a big bass drum with muffled sticks, around which they squatted in a circle while the drum lay flat on the ground between them.

Each day, on opening the ceremonies, some noted chief would make an oration. One, by Pretty Bird, was strikingly like a Roman Senator as pictured in classic paintings. He stood more than six feet in height and, with his blanket draped about his shoulders as only an Indian can carry one with grace, his attitudes and gestures, as well as his language and delivery, were superbly impressive. The President of the Indian association sponsoring the big event was William Spotted Tail. He was son of the celebrated chief of old days who was assassinated by Crow Dog, whose daughter Walking Crow Woman, was present to join in the celebration. She was about seventy and, when encountered in the Pine-Ridge-section village, she was engaged in preparing a puppy dog feast. On hearing the click of the kodak she became indignant and threatened the intruder with dire consequences. But when she discovered that he was a member of her own tribe, she relented and invited him to the banquet which would be ready at dusk. She told the story of her noted father and brought out from her tepee the knife he had used in lifting the scalp of the famed chief at Rosebud. It had thirteen notches on the handle— record of his bravery in the troublous war-times. She ex- hibited her grandmother's valued wampum belt of beads, some of which were the crude iridescent ones turned out by the Mandans described by Lewis and Clark who stayed with them over the winter in 1804; others were specimens from the Jesuits' visits in the early exploration days.

Not far away was the camp of Bear Dog, a brother of the famous Hollow Horn Bear—last of that family of chiefs. He possessed the original Peace medal presented to his grand- father by President George Washington; it bore the date 1789 and was worn by the three succeeding generations of chiefs, and lastly by his brother, who gave it to him at his death, many years ago.

Near by was met Good Face, a survivor of the Custer fight, who had been with Buffalo Bill in his tour of Europe, and of whom the Farm superintendent said, "He is the finest man on the Reservation." Frank Goings, the scout, Jim Grass, Kills-Close-to-the-Lodge, White-Rabbit and Nancy Sitting Bull, were encountered while on a walk through the Sioux district villages.

In the midst of the solemnities of the dance rituals, a po- litical candidate intruded with his retinue of office-holders and moving picture men. The performers were jostled by the rude camera-carriers and news-reel fiends, who, in the mad struggle to obtain records of this notable event, climbed upon the roof of their frail "wickiup" and crushed the timbers. They pawed over those who sat in its shade regardless of manners or results.

Top—Showing dress of Sun Dance performers in certain features of the last Sun
 Dance of the Sioux, 1928. All brilliant colors, both body and regalia.

Center—Vice President Curtis being posed for photo during the Sun Dance pro-
 ceedings for use of the movies and Sunday illustrated editions.

Bottom—During the recess of the ceremony of the Sun Dance.

The candidate was required to have his picture taken, with the chief in regalia, in the act of grasping his hand in welcome, for propaganda in the elections then coming on. The chief had to be urged, but finally yielded, and the photo was made. It appeared in the Sunday supplements through-out the eastern cities, where it is presumed it had its expected favorable effect in the ballot-box, but it had a decidedly adverse result when the Indian ballots were counted in the west.

With the unwelcome interruption, the performers quit abruptly and refused to complete the afternoon ceremonies, whereupon the Winnebagoes took control of the arena and started a war-dance in which other tribes joined. As twilight came on all the various tribes joined in the excitement, until the multitudes covered the vacant ground all around. The larger the crowd became the faster they danced and the louder the yelping war cries resounded over the bordering hills. Looking on from a higher altitude this moving mass of humanity offered a unique spectacle—one never seen before, and most likely never to be seen again. It was the biggest war-dance ever held. A ranchman who was looking on remarked that he was accustomed to big things in the big western country, but the scene before him was, in its dimension and import, astounding.

It was with a feeling of sadness and humiliation that we entered and took part in the ceremony with the old chiefs for the last sun dance of the Sioux, knowing as all did that it would be the farewell between friends—almost half a century of friendly intercourse and mutual understanding now to end forever. A last ceremonial smoke with the old warriors in the Council tepee, hearty handshake to each, and we were off for a drive across the Indian's home lands, west to the border. We wanted to see how they now lived as compared with the long ago.

From the hill-top three miles out a backward glance re-vealed the breaking up of the grand conclave we had par-ticipated in; it was the clearing of the stage after the fall of the curtain on a notable national tragedy; it was as if there had been performed the last sad rites at the grave of stricken brothers. It was the end of the old-time Indian days.

We were staging in the Rosebud Country, last home-land of the red folks and of the Sioux. Their lonely and forbidding huts were in evidence along the way; ground-floor, flimsy log cabins, with one door, a window and mud roof; their farms bare, parched and treeless, utterly devoid of growing or growable things. Here they eke out a miserable existence with their little families, hopeless and hungry, a forlorn fruit-less life. Occasionally is seen a small white-painted church, always surrounded by a large burying ground filled with graves and marked with little wood crosses, glaring proof of the neglect suffered by them under the restricted reserva-tion system.

Past an Indian trading store, kept by a white man. Always where there is profit it goes to the whites from the pockets of the reds. Up and down the highway runs over land, the natural haunt of the rattler and the coyote, shunned by birds, beasts and white men.

Once the regulation log shanty was seen on the crest of a barren ridge, alongside of which was a canvass tepee, all sur-rounded by broken-down wagons, parts of mower and rake, showing that the owner had tried to live as regulations re-quired. It was plain that farming could not succeed on such land, yet he was not permitted to leave his allotted location; and so he had set up a flimsy canvass-lodge where he could at least have fresh air and sunshine which the white man's kind of log hut did not supply.

Then over barren ridges, past He Dog's village, where there was another trading store, passing and meeting but three motor cars in a half-day's journey. Farther west the lands improve slightly. Some of it is devoted to flax, and sometimes wheat crops mature, but the crops this year had failed on account of excessive frosts, hail, and the withering hot winds. Here and there were evidences that ranchers tried to get a start, and had failed, on lands leased from the Indian— further proof that the red man is forced to live where the white man cannot.

A stop for lunch at a white man's town, census 100, where they raised cattle and had a court house, stores and a post-office, all forty miles from a railroad. While this year's crop was a failure, they were hopeful that boom days would come again.

Another long leg of the journey over this lifeless and uninviting country,—waterless, dusty and dreary, and the historic Wounded Knee massacre site and the trading store— became a stop for gasoline and oil. A glance over the monument and massacre grounds only added to the cheerlessness and the depressed feeling resulting from the last few days' experiences in the Indian country. John Cross Dog, with his wife and a few merchandise packages, and their little boy, were taken on board the car for a ride towards their home beyond Pine Ridge.

Between Wounded Knee creek and Pine Ridge agency the country improved; there was wheat harvested from it and other evidences of human habitation and practical farming.

A short stop was made at the agency office to ask about the chief. He had started to the sun dance, but the dilapidated

old Ford broke down somewhere in the Bad Lands section and
he never arrived. He now had gone to visit friends at the
Standing Rock district in North Dakota; he wanted to visit
Sitting Bull's grave there. Thunderbull came to shake, with
his cheerful "How Kola," and then a snapshot was made of
Red Cloud's monument and grave; the start was then made
on the last lap.

The way was rough to the river valley, where the John
Cross Dog family was let out with their bundles to be carried,
with the child, to their lonely log shack back among the chalk-
cliffs—somewhere. A little white church with its well-filled
"cemetery" was passed as the road led into the foothills of the
Bad Lands country. It was "desolation" for a long way, but
there was water, and as animal and human life cannot exist
long without water they tolerate the worthless barrens in order to be within reach of it. Oglala was reached—a trading
store and hitching rack for cowboys' horses, and a filling pump
for the motor cars. During the stop for gas our old friend
John Sitting Bull came out. It was an unexpected meeting,
and the driver kindly delayed long enough to permit a short
visit and a close-up of the adopted son of the famous chief.
Dressed in cheap overalls and slouch hat, he seemed in good
health, and by sign language referred to a visit to the home
of the white brother some twenty years ago. John can neither
speak nor hear, but in facial expression is a good counterpart
of the old Medicine man.

As the road swings out of the valley and gradually ascends
the long slopes of the treeless mountains forming the divide
between the White and Cheyenne rivers, void of human habi-
tations and, so far as could be observed, likewise of bird or
animal life, there appeared near the river a band of wild horses
which stampeded at sight of the automobile. It was the only

sign of living creatures for a long distance.

The sun was descending behind the higher peaks of the Black Hills in the far distance as the western line of the Pine Ridge Reservation on the "divide" was passed. Harney Peak could be identified at the north, and soon the grade was turn-ing downward toward the Cheyenne River valley. On the western slope the land was better. Here and there were farms, and apples grew; fences appeared and domestic live-stock was in evidence along the way. A railroad! The blast of a locomotive's whistle came to remind us we had reached the land of the white man.

Two hundred miles through Indian country; two hundred miles of desolation. Indian Country because white men would not, could not, do not live in it,—except those who profit from the misfortunes and sufferings of the conquered and dying race of First Americans.

.   .   .   .

On returning to the east a current magazine was delivered for attention to a marked article appearing in it, viz.:

"Gaunt poverty is in almost every Indian reservation today, and so is hunger and so also is contagious disease, and so is complete subjugation of person and property of the Indian. Because of their valor in the World War the Indian was made free by law—they assume—they are entitled to the same treatment as white folks get."

"He cannot sell his own land; he cannot worship in his own way; he cannot rear his own children. If he leaves the reservation without permission he can be thrown into jail with ball and chain on his body and held any length of time without trial—no counsel, no right of appeal. The agent can do as he pleases—recognizes no superior. The Indian is a slave and a pauper in a country which abolished slavery after the bloodiest war in history, to do so."

To know from experience of many years, to see, to hear and feel at first hand, the truth of our terrible national crime, and to realize the cold-hearted indifference of Congress and the officials responsible for these conditions, is to wonder if there is a Law of Justice.

Is it any wonder they doubt the power of the white man's prayer? What has the white man's God done for them? And we hear in reply: "Ever since we heard of the white man's Manitou we have been persecuted, robbed, cheated, debased, diseased and rum-ruined by white men; nothing they told us but has proven false. What right have we to believe in him or in his God?"

To one who understands, no apology, explanation or "reason" is necessary to appreciate the gathering together of the northwest tribes, at great inconvenience and suffering, to pay a last tribute of reverence to the only God they know and understand and believe in,—by joining in the sacred ceremonies at "The Last Sun Dance of the Sioux."

The Crazy Horse Carbine. Springfield—model of 1873. Old Sioux bow and arrows Indians say was used in the Custer fight. Original Washington medal, 1789, from Bear Dog, brother of the late Chief Hollow Horn Bear. This medal was presented to their grandfather when Chief and worn by the son and grandson chiefs, successors to the original. War Shirt of Chief Flying Hawk decorated with scalp-locks. War Bonnet owned by Chief Rain-in-the-Face.

CPSIA information can be obtained
at www.ICGtesting.com
Printed in the USA
BVHW030238090819
555487BV00002B/413/P